How to Analyze the Works of

GEORGIA
O'KEEFFE

by Michael Fallon

ABDO
Publishing Company

Essential Critiques

How to Analyze the Works of

GEORGIA O'KEEFFE

by Michael Fallon

Content Consultant: Joan Rothfuss, adjunct faculty,
College of Visual Arts

Credits

Published by ABDO Publishing Company, 8000 West 78th Street, Edina,
Minnesota 55439. Copyright © 2011 by Abdo Consulting Group, Inc.
International copyrights reserved in all countries. No part of this book may be
reproduced in any form without written permission from the publisher.
The Essential Library™ is a trademark and logo of ABDO Publishing Company.

Printed in the United States of America,
North Mankato, Minnesota
062010
092010

 THIS BOOK CONTAINS AT LEAST 10% RECYCLED MATERIALS.

Special thanks to Laura Wertheim, Contributing Author for chapters 4, 9, and 1
Editor: Mari Kesselring
Copy Editor: Paula Lewis
Interior Design and Production: Marie Tupy
Cover Design: Marie Tupy

Library of Congress Cataloging-in-Publication Data
Fallon, Michael, 1966-
  How to analyze the works of Georgia O'Keeffe / Michael Fallon.
    p. cm. — (Essential critiques)
  Includes bibliographical references and index.
  ISBN 978-1-61613-535-5
1. O'Keeffe, Georgia, 1887-1986—Criticism and interpretation—Juvenile
literature. 2. Art appreciation—Juvenile literature. 3. Art criticism—Juvenile
literature. I. O'Keeffe, Georgia, 1887-1986. II. Title.
  ND237.O5F35 2010
  759.13—dc22
                                    2010015883

Table of Contents

Chapter 1   Introduction to Critiques   6

Chapter 2   A Closer Look at Georgia O'Keeffe   13

Chapter 3   An Overview of *Evening Star No. V*   27

Chapter 4   How to Apply Formalist Criticism to *Evening Star No. V*   33

Chapter 5   An Overview of *The Black Iris*   45

Chapter 6   How to Apply Feminist Criticism to *The Black Iris*   51

Chapter 7   An Overview of *Red Hills with White Shell*   61

Chapter 8   How to Apply Biographical Criticism to *Red Hills with White Shell*   67

Chapter 9   An Overview of *Pelvis Series Red with Yellow*   79

Chapter 10   How to Apply Structuralism to *Pelvis Series Red with Yellow*   85

You Critique It   96

Timeline   98

Glossary   100

Bibliography of Works and Criticism   102

Resources   104

Source Notes   106

Index   109

About the Author   112

Chapter

1

Introduction to Critiques

What Is Critical Theory?

What do you usually do when you visit an art museum? You probably enjoy seeing the works of different painters, sculptors, and other artists. You see the many ways the artists have expressed themselves through their creations. Certain works of art might catch your eye and invite you to study them more closely. Yet these are only a few of many possible ways of understanding and appreciating a work of art. What if you are interested in delving more deeply? You might want to learn more about the artist and how his or her personal background is reflected in the artwork. Or you might want to examine what the artwork says about society—how it depicts the roles of women and minorities,

for example. If so, you have entered the realm of critical theory.

Critical theory helps you learn how various works of art, literature, music, theater, film, and other endeavors either support or challenge the way society behaves. Critical theory is the evaluation and interpretation of a work using different philosophies, or schools of thought. Critical theory can be used to understand all types of cultural productions.

There are many different critical theories. If you are analyzing a work of art, each theory asks you to look at the work from a different perspective. Some theories address social issues, while others focus on the artist's life, the technique used to create the artwork, or the time period in which the artwork was created. For example, the critical theory that asks how an artist's life affected the work is called biographical criticism. Other common schools of criticism include historical criticism, feminist criticism, and psychological criticism. New Criticism examines a work solely within the context of the work itself.

What Is the Purpose of Critical Theory?

Critical theory can open your mind to new ways of thinking. It can help you evaluate a work of art from a new perspective, directing your attention to issues and messages you may not otherwise recognize in a work.

For example, applying feminist criticism to an artwork may make you aware of female stereotypes perpetuated in the work. Applying a critical theory to a work helps you learn about the person who created it or the society that enjoyed it. You can explore how the artwork is perceived by current cultures.

How Do You Apply Critical Theory?

You conduct a critique when you use a critical theory to examine and question a work. The theory you choose is a lens through which you can view the work, or a springboard for asking questions about the work. Applying a critical theory helps you to think critically about the work. You are free to question the work and make an assertion about it. If you choose to examine a work of art using biographical theory, for example, you want to know how the artist's personal background or education inspired or shaped the work. You could explore why the artist was drawn to the subject, theme, or technique of the work of art. For instance, were there events in the artist's past that might have caused him or her to choose a certain topic?

Forming a Thesis

Ask your question and find answers in the work or other related materials. Then you can create a thesis. The thesis is the key point in your critique. It is your argument about the work based on the tenets, or beliefs, of the theory you are using. For example, if you are using biographical theory to ask how the artist's life inspired the work, your thesis

How to Make a Thesis Statement

In a critique, a thesis statement typically appears at the end of the introductory paragraph. It is usually only one sentence long and states the author's main idea.

How to Support a Thesis Statement

A critique should include several arguments. Arguments support a thesis claim. An argument is one or two sentences long and is supported by evidence from the work being discussed.

Organize the arguments into paragraphs. These paragraphs make up the body of the critique.

could be worded as follows: Artist Teng Xiong, raised in refugee camps in southeast Asia, drew upon her experiences to create the painting *No Home for Me*.

Providing Evidence

Once you have formed a thesis, you must provide evidence to support it. Evidence might take the form of examples from the work itself, such as the subject or technique. Articles about the work of art or personal interviews with the artist might also support your ideas. You may wish to address what other critics have written about the work. Quotes from these individuals may help support your claim. If you find any quotes or examples that contradict your thesis, you will need to create an argument against them. For instance: Many critics have asserted that the dark colors in *No Home for Me* convey the depressing reality of living in refugee camps. However, the painting clearly focuses on tender, positive moments between members of the refugee community.

In This Book

In this book, you will read overviews that describe famous works of art by artist Georgia O'Keeffe, each followed by a critique. Each critique will use one theory and apply it to one work. Critical thinking sections will give you a chance to consider other theses and questions about the work. Did you agree with the author's application of the theory? What other questions are raised by the thesis and its arguments? You can also find out what other critics think about each particular artwork. Then, in the You Critique It section in the final pages of this book, you will have an opportunity to create your own critique.

Look for the Guides

Throughout the chapters that analyze the works, thesis statements have been highlighted. The box next to the thesis helps explain what questions are being raised about the work. Supporting arguments have been underlined. The boxes next to the arguments help explain how these points support the thesis. Look for these guides throughout each critique.

Georgia O'Keeffe in 1953

Chapter

2

A Closer Look at Georgia O'Keeffe

Georgia O'Keeffe was an American artist. She was born in a farmhouse near the town of Sun Prairie, Wisconsin, on November 15, 1887. Her parents, Francis and Ida O'Keeffe, were dairy farmers. Georgia was the first girl and the second of seven children in the O'Keeffe family. Most of the children showed artistic talent when they were young.

Education for women was important in the O'Keeffe family. When Georgia was young, she attended the local one-room schoolhouse and received art instruction from Sarah Mann, an amateur painter. When Georgia was 11 years old, she began to take drawing lessons at home with two of her younger sisters. She particularly enjoyed making still-life and landscape paintings.

In 1901, Georgia started high school at Sacred Heart Academy in Madison, Wisconsin. But in 1902, the O'Keeffe family faced economic difficulties. The family moved to Williamsburg, Virginia, but Georgia stayed in Wisconsin with her aunt. She later rejoined her family in 1903 and attended high school at the Chatham Episcopal Institute, a boarding school in Virginia. She graduated from high school in 1905.

Artistic Training

After high school, O'Keeffe attended art schools in Chicago and New York City. Her family was still short on money, but they believed O'Keeffe had the potential to be a self-supporting artist. In New York, while studying at the Art Students League, O'Keeffe thrived. She had many artist friends and enjoyed the competition of other artists. She became enraptured by the excitement of the big city and fascinated by modern art.

In 1908, O'Keeffe painted a simplified still-life image of a dead rabbit lying near a copper pot. This painting won the Art Students League's prestigious

William Merritt Chase Award. She was given an opportunity to study that summer at an art colony in upstate New York. Afterward, O'Keeffe did not have enough money to continue living in New York City. She returned to Virginia to live with her family, whose economic situation had worsened.

Discouraged about money and her stalled art career, O'Keeffe eventually moved to Chicago. She found a job there as a commercial illustrator and was able to send money back home to help her family. Although her work in Chicago was difficult and tiring, she stayed at this job for two years. Eventually, O'Keeffe became discouraged that she could not find time to create her own paintings. She returned home to Virginia once again in 1911, depressed and sick from the measles.

In 1912, with her sister Anita's encouragement, O'Keeffe took a summer class for teachers at the University of Virginia. Her instructor, Alon Bement, taught her new ways to think about art. Bement was a follower of his teacher, Arthur Wesley Dow, the famous American art educator. Dow published his ideas about art in 1899 in *Composition: A Series of Exercises in Art Structure for the Use of Students and Teachers*. The book focuses on Dow's ideas for putting together images by using lines, masses, and colors. Above everything, Dow stressed to artists the need to create harmony in their images. Because of this, he thought composition was the most important skill for artists to develop. He believed that once artists had mastered composition, it would be easier for them to create art. Bement encouraged O'Keeffe to express herself freely and to invent her own patterns and compositions in paint. Excited by new possibilities, O'Keeffe worked with Bement for several years. She once again found inspiration to paint.

O'Keeffe had learned from Bement that artists should not try to copy nature. She had also learned that an artist should think primarily about formal elements such as line, mass, and color. This was in opposition to the way most artists had created art in the nineteenth century. O'Keeffe began painting by focusing mostly on elements of composition. In 1916, she was offered a job as an art teacher at West Texas State Normal College. She moved to the small prairie town of Canyon, Texas, to begin work as a teacher in the fall of 1916.

Early Artistic Career

O'Keeffe at age 29 around the time she started teaching art

In 1916, O'Keeffe also eagerly began making new works of art. A few months after she arrived in Texas, she mailed a roll of her new charcoal drawings to Anita Pollitzer, a friend in New York. O'Keeffe told her friend not to show the drawings to anyone, so Pollitzer opened the tube behind a locked door. Looking at the paintings, she was "struck by their aliveness."[1] Pollitzer was surprised at how exciting O'Keeffe's art had become.

Pollitzer decided, despite O'Keeffe's wishes, she could not keep her friend's drawings to herself. She showed them to Alfred Stieglitz, a photographic artist and gallery owner. In the early twentieth century, many people did not take women seriously as artists. Alfred Stieglitz's approach to female artists was a rare exception to this attitude. He believed females experienced life differently from males. He thought these differences enabled female artists to express vividly personal visions.

When Stieglitz saw O'Keeffe's drawings, he immediately admired the sense of expression and freedom. He thought the bold lines and shapes were the work of an intensely expressive woman. Interestingly, when O'Keeffe created these drawings, she told a friend her intent was to express a woman's feelings. Stieglitz told Pollitzer he would like to show them in his gallery. When Pollitzer wrote to O'Keeffe about what she had done, O'Keeffe was not angry, but excited that Stieglitz wanted to show her art. The interest that Stieglitz, who had a reputation for appreciating avant-garde art, showed toward O'Keeffe's art encouraged her. O'Keeffe's first solo art show took place at Stieglitz's 291 Gallery in April 1917. Unfortunately, O'Keeffe could not attend the show because she was still teaching in Texas.

The First Show

O'Keeffe's first show at the 291 Gallery caused a stir among the public. Critics, artists, and others filled the gallery to see the work of an unknown female art teacher. Many were shocked by what they saw. Although the drawings were abstract, they conveyed a powerful sensuality that disturbed many people. Stieglitz saw nothing wrong with art that expressed sexual feeling. He believed artists should have full creative freedom to express what they wanted. Despite some of the controversy, critics who saw the show mostly deemed it a success.

In May, at the end of the school year in Texas, O'Keeffe took a train to New York and made a surprise visit to the 291 Gallery. Her show had already been taken down, but Stieglitz was so excited to see her that he hung every picture back up in the gallery for her to see.

Back to New York

A year later, in June of 1918, O'Keeffe moved to New York City. Stieglitz soon fell in love with the younger artist, even though he was married. He separated from his wife, Emmeline, later that year. After his divorce in 1924, Stieglitz and O'Keeffe were married. They lived together somewhat happily for many years.

Beginning in 1923, Stieglitz organized annual exhibitions of O'Keeffe's work at several different New York galleries. By the mid-1920s, O'Keeffe had become a well-known artist. She often transformed her subjects into dramatic and emotionally charged images that were both abstract and representational.

By 1929, the demands of producing enough art for the annual shows Stieglitz organized began to wear on O'Keeffe. Also, she began to feel stifled in New York. She decided to travel in order to find more inspiration from nature for her paintings. In May 1929, O'Keeffe took a train to Taos,

New Mexico, to visit a close friend. She also visited
Santa Fe and Albuquerque and felt inspiration
returning to her. Soon after her arrival, O'Keeffe

O'Keeffe
married Alfred
Stieglitz.

was invited to spend the summer at a ranch outside Taos. She made a number of paintings of the things she saw while she stayed there.

Between 1929 and 1949, O'Keeffe spent part of nearly every year in New Mexico. Usually, she stayed in the region for the summer before returning to New York. In the summer of 1934, after O'Keeffe suffered a nervous breakdown, she visited Ghost Ranch, north of Abiquiu in New Mexico. She was inspired by the multicolored cliffs around the ranch and decided she wanted to live there. In 1940, she purchased a house on Ghost Ranch. Meanwhile, her reputation as an artist had continued to grow. She had major retrospective shows at the Art Institute of Chicago in 1943 and at the Museum of Modern Art in Manhattan in 1946. Then, while O'Keeffe was spending the summer of 1946 in New Mexico, her husband, Alfred Stieglitz, suddenly took ill. She flew to New York, and he passed away on July 13, 1946. In 1949, O'Keeffe moved to New Mexico permanently.

Contributions and Awards

O'Keeffe made many contributions to the art community in the United States throughout her

life. In the early and middle parts of the twentieth century, O'Keeffe played a large role in bringing American art to Europe. At the time, Europeans were not known for their interest in American art. Europeans looked down on the art and culture of a country they considered too youthful and naïve

O'Keeffe's studio at Ghost Ranch

to be important. O'Keeffe's ability to help break through European snobbery enhanced her historical reputation.

Also, at the time O'Keeffe worked as an artist, there were few women artists who had much artistic influence. In the 1930s, an art critic called her "the foremost woman-painter of the world."[2] O'Keeffe is said to have possessed a remarkable determination to succeed. This determination helped her be an innovative artist.

Because of her popularity and talent, O'Keeffe was awarded many honors during her lifetime. In 1962, O'Keeffe was elected to the 50-member American Academy of Arts and Letters. In the fall of 1970, the Whitney Museum of American Art mounted a major retrospective exhibition of her work, bringing it to a new generation of art lovers. In 1977, President Gerald R. Ford awarded O'Keeffe with the Presidential Medal of Freedom.

Later Life

O'Keeffe became increasingly frail in her 90s and started to lose her eyesight. She began to work more with ceramics and pottery. But, remarkably, she continued to paint until just a few weeks before

she died on March 6, 1986. She was 98 years old. Today, the Georgia O'Keeffe Museum in Santa Fe, New Mexico, owns a large number of her paintings and other works, helping to maintain O'Keeffe's enduring artistic legacy.

An exhibition of O'Keeffe's work in 2003

Evening Star No. V, 1917

Chapter
3

An Overview of
Evening Star No. V

In 1917, O'Keeffe painted *Evening Star No. V.* This was before she moved from Texas to New York. It was during a period of great change in the visual arts in the United States. Modernism had attracted the imagination of artists and certain lovers of art.

O'Keeffe made ten watercolor paintings of the evening star. As the title of the painting suggests, *Evening Star No. V* is the fifth of ten paintings on the same subject. *Evening Star No. V* is a small image, approximately 9 x 12 in. (22 x 30 cm), that is painted on paper and mounted on board.

The Evening Star

Although the image is abstract, O'Keeffe thought of the evening star when she made the painting. In late afternoons, after she finished teaching her classes, O'Keeffe often walked away from the small town of Canyon, Texas, where she lived. In Canyon, there were no paved roads, fences, nor trees. "It was like the ocean," O'Keeffe later wrote, "but it was wide, wide land."[1]

The evening star is actually the planet Venus, which usually appears in the western sky after the sun has set. O'Keeffe was fascinated and excited by this spot of light. She would walk and watch the sunset and the bright evening star. Afterward, she would return to her studio and paint what she remembered.

A Modern Painting

During the time O'Keeffe painted her evening star paintings, modernist ideas were changing the way artists in the United States and Europe thought about creating art. No longer were artists simply considered interpreters of reality and culture; they were inventors of their own new realities.

Artists in Europe redefined art forms in radical new ways. Pablo Picasso and Georges Braque created Cubism. A group of mostly German artists called the Blue Rider group, led by Wassily Kandinsky, pushed Expressionist art more and more into abstraction. Many other European artists, such as Henri Matisse, Robert Delaunay, and Piet Mondrian, developed new art movements such as Fauvism, orphism, and neo-plasticism.

Despite the influence of U.S. teachers such as Alon Bement, modernism was slow in reaching the United States. Eventually, several decades after the movement started, the United States was exposed to modernist art at the 1913 Armory Show in New York City. This exhibition displayed the art of Impressionist, Fauvist, and Cubist artists from Europe. These paintings startled many U.S. viewers who were accustomed to more representational art, or art that depicts recognizable objects or people. However, many U.S. artists, such as Alfred Stieglitz and his friends, were influenced by the radical new ideas. Modernism slowly gained popularity in the United States over the next two decades. In time, the trends of modernism would dominate American art for much of the twentieth century.

A Unique Application of Modern Art

O'Keeffe understood modern art to be less about painting reality and more about creating expressive, colorful, and well-composed images that contained a spiritual truth. Because of this, O'Keeffe experimented with modernism in her evening star paintings. In these images, she started with a yellow ball of light that represents the star. She placed it higher on the canvas, as if to show that it was in the sky. She focused not on the way the star really looked in nature, but on expressing something emotional she felt about the star. She painted whatever abstract shapes and expressive colors came to her mind. She took care to focus on the composition of the image and how the shapes fit together.

In all of the evening star paintings, O'Keeffe painted imagery that was both abstract and representational. *Evening Star No. V* does not look like the surface appearance of the natural world. It is an abstracted and somewhat mystical version of nature. In this way, O'Keeffe mimicked European modernist artists of the time such as Kandinsky and Matisse. At the same time, O'Keeffe worked to create her own personal style and manner of

painting that was both similar to and different from the modernist painters she admired.

The 1913 Armory Show in New York City exposed many Americans to modernist art that was already popular in Europe.

Formalists study a work's color, line, space, mass, scale, and composition.

4

How to Apply Formalist Criticism to *Evening Star No. V*

What Is Formalist Criticism?

Even before the Middle Ages, the purpose of art was to create the illusion of three-dimensionality. With the rise of modern art, artists began to reject the idea that art should be illusionistic. They suggested it should convey, rather than conceal, its two-dimensionality. In other words, modern art moved away from representing recognizable objects and people and toward abstraction.

Formalist criticism grew directly out of the rise of modern art. Art critics who used formalist theories were very supportive of the developments of modern art. They praised modern art for emphasizing flatness and two-dimensionality and for not seeking to imitate real objects or people in the world.

Formalist criticism may sound complicated, but it is one of the most basic theoretical approaches to take. Unlike some other theories, you do not need to have any prior knowledge of the artwork you analyze. Formalists believe that everything you need to understand a work of art is contained within the work itself. Formalists also seek to avoid projecting their own beliefs or experiences onto a work. They believe an objective analysis is possible.

On the most basic level, a formal analysis consists of describing what one sees in a work using precise, art historical vocabulary. But, there is a bit more to this approach than that. In the end, formalists want to suggest what the overall visual effect of the piece they are analyzing is. In a formalist analysis, one must consider color, line, space, mass, scale, and composition.

Applying Formalist Criticism to *Evening Star No. V*

O'Keeffe's watercolor from 1917, entitled *Evening Star No. V*, is an example of abstract, rather than representational, American modern art. This work is based on O'Keeffe's observation of a real thing—the night sky— and the work is suggestive of the atmosphere and landscape she is drawing

from. However, O'Keeffe significantly stylized her subject. O'Keeffe's artistic intentions and the context in which she created the work are not relevant from a formalist perspective.

O'Keeffe observed the sunset in Canyon, Texas, to create *Evening Star No. V.*

In *Evening Star No. V*, O'Keeffe uses color, more than any other formal element, to create a vivid and theatrical compositional field. The contrasting qualities of the colors create a tension and drama between them. Furthermore, the way in which O'Keeffe applies color, in flat geometrical bands, emphasizes the two-dimensionality of the paper. In *Evening Star No. V*, O'Keeffe draws attention to color, line, and paint application to create a purely abstract yet emotionally evocative composition.

O'Keeffe uses color to create tension in *Evening Star No. V*. She contrasts bright and warm reds, oranges, and yellows with deep, cool, stormy blues and grays. The colors are arranged in spiral bands that increase in intensity toward the outside of the spiral. The relative lightness or darkness of the colors also impacts the effect the color has on the composition. Generally, colors with more black express a more brooding or dramatic atmosphere, while colors with more white express a lighter and calmer atmosphere. In *Evening Star No. V*, the yellow is lighter, while the blues are darker. So the composition is neither entirely brooding nor entirely calm. Rather, there is a tension between these two atmospheres. This tension is exaggerated by contrasting not only light and dark colors, but also warm and cool colors, and saturated and unsaturated colors.

O'Keeffe also uses color in *Evening Star No. V* to create the effect of energy spreading outward from a central point. This use of color creates overall motion in this composition. In the painting, the more intense and darker blues surround a series of brighter and warmer spiral bands of color that radiate inward. The red circle and tail is more saturated than the orange circle within it, which

Argument Two

The author is continuing to address how O'Keeffe uses color in *Evening Star No. V*. The author is adding to the previous paragraph's examination of color in the painting. But here, the author focuses on color creating motion: "O'Keeffe also uses color in *Evening Star No. V* to create the effect of energy spreading outward from a central point. This use of color creates overall motion in this composition."

are more saturated than the yellow circle within them, which is closest to the center of the spiral. A small unpainted void is at the center. The increasing intensity of the warmth and saturation of the color bands toward the outside of the spiral gives the composition a radiating quality.

<u>Painterly compositions often convey dimension by means of a play between light and dark and seek to deemphasize and conceal lines; they are meant to depict something specific like a landscape or person. In contrast, O'Keeffe's composition in *Evening Star No. V* appears flat and two-dimensional.</u> The composition is organized around a central point, from which increasingly saturated and warm circular bands of color radiate. These bands of color appear flat and smooth and emphasize the picture plane rather than create an illusion of dimensionality. Unpainted strips of white paper separate these bands of color. The white space reminds viewers

Argument Three

In this point, the author continues to discuss the color in the painting, but he also introduces how line is used to create an abstract painting. He starts to reveal how these elements make the painting abstract: "Painterly compositions often convey dimension by means of a play between light and dark and seek to deemphasize and conceal lines; they are meant to depict something specific like a landscape or person. In contrast, O'Keeffe's composition in *Evening Star No. V* appears flat and two-dimensional."

they are looking at a two-dimensional surface and not a three-dimensional space.

<u>The manner in which O'Keeffe applies the paint to the paper draws attention to the painting as a work of art rather than a simple reproduction of a scene.</u> There are places in the composition where the blue paint bleeds into the red paint, which makes viewers aware that this

O'Keeffe's use of color in *Evening Star No. V* creates tension.

Argument Four

The author is now proving the final part of the thesis. He concludes that the painting is abstract due to how the paint has been applied to the paper: "The manner in which O'Keeffe applies the paint to the paper draws attention to the painting as a work of art rather than a simple reproduction of a scene."

is a watercolor painting. Unlike works of art that seek to conceal the materials from which they were made, this painting makes the materials visible. The application of the watercolors draws attention to itself, thereby exposing the medium. In other words, the swirling colors look like paint, not like objects in the world.

Conclusion

This final paragraph is the conclusion of the critique. It sums up the author's arguments and partially restates the original thesis, which has now been argued and supported with evidence.

From a formal perspective, O'Keeffe's composition is not a clear reproduction of an evening star. The red spiral and tail do not make reference to a comet; the play of blues and grays do not resemble the clouds and the sky. Instead, *Evening Star No. V* is an abstraction of the star that attempts to convey O'Keeffe's personal emotional connection with this scene.

Thinking Critically about *Evening Star No. V*

Now it's your turn to assess the critique. Consider these questions:

1. The thesis argues that the painting is abstract. Do you agree? What do you think makes it an abstract painting? What might dismiss it as abstract?

2. The thesis also claims that the choice of paint conveys emotions. Do you think that is true? Why or why not?

3. In looking at the composition, what other elements from the work seem to convey emotion?

4. What was the most interesting argument made? What was the weakest? How did the evidence from the painting help prove the arguments? What other evidence might you use?

Other Approaches

What you have just read is one possible way to apply a formalist approach to a critique of *Evening Star No. V*. Remember that a formalist critique focuses solely on the elements in the painting. What are some other ways experts have approached it? Two alternative approaches follow. The first approach focuses on other aspects of the painting not mentioned in this critique that help to create an abstract painting. The other approach claims that the painting is, in fact, representational rather than abstract.

Watercolor Helps Make the Painting Abstract

Some critics have argued that in addition to the application of the paint making the work abstract, the use of watercolor also helps to give the painting a modern, abstract look. The argument is that the watercolor paint flows across the page, bringing more attention to the medium than to what the painter's subject may be.

A thesis statement for this argument might be: O'Keeffe's use of watercolor paint in *Evening Star No. V* helps her create an abstract painting.

The Painting Is Representational

Clement Greenberg, an influential American art critic, is closely associated with American modern art. He advocated forcefully for pure formalism. During a 1946 exhibition of O'Keeffe's work in New York, Greenberg was very critical and claimed that O'Keeffe's work was too representational and not abstract enough. He said her work was only "pseudo-modern."[1]

The thesis statement for Greenberg's argument might be: O'Keeffe's *Evening Star No. V* relates closely enough to an actual evening star that it is still a representational painting and not a truly abstract work.

The Black Iris, 1926

5

An Overview of
The Black Iris

Soon after her arrival in New York,
O'Keeffe began working with oil
paint instead of watercolor. Her art
slowly began to evolve. Between 1918
and 1923, she produced a number
of colorful and dynamic abstract
paintings. For example, in 1919,
O'Keeffe used oils in *Red & Orange
Streak*. It is comprised of a curving
stripe of orange color that sweeps across a dark
background. Another, smaller horizontal stripe
of red cuts across the upper portion of the dark
background. This painting could be a landscape,
or it could just be a series of abstract shapes. The
use of oil paint, in this and other works, makes the
paintings seem even more real and tactile.

The Flower Paintings

In the early and mid-1920s, O'Keeffe began making very large-scale paintings of natural forms up close, as if seen through a magnifying lens. While this was a shift from the more abstract paintings she made in the late 1910s, there were still many similarities. In particular, O'Keeffe was known for her love of certain shapes in her more abstract paintings. She included swirl shapes in many of her works. These look like spiraling whirlpools of color. O'Keeffe repeated this shape in many of her paintings. She also often painted several other shapes, such as curved forms like slits of flower petals or tubular-like holes in the center of an iris.

In the flower paintings, O'Keeffe made use of many of the favorite shapes that appear in her more abstract paintings. It is very possible that O'Keeffe sought out flowers to use as still-life models because she saw in them many of the shapes she loved to paint. She said she liked to paint flowers as still-life paintings because it was always easy to find flowers.

In 1924, O'Keeffe painted her first large-scale flower painting, *Petunia, No. 2*. It includes a stripe

O'Keeffe painted large images of many different types of flowers, including petunias.

shape, much as in *Red & Orange Streak*, except the stripe is green. It could be interpreted as an abstract leaf or branch. The pink petunia flowers in this painting are more recognizable. They appear soft and delicate, but are very large and seen close up.

Between 1924 and 1930, O'Keeffe regularly painted large images of simple garden flowers such as roses, petunias, poppies, camellias, sunflowers, and begonias. She painted each flower in oil paint on a large canvas. But instead of painting a naturalistic or realistic image, O'Keeffe increasingly painted the flowers as simple compositions of bright shapes and vivid colors.

The Black Iris

O'Keeffe painted *The Black Iris* in New York in 1926. *The Black Iris* is one of several versions that O'Keeffe painted of the black iris flower. It is painted in oil on a 9 x 7 in. (22.9 x 17.8 cm) canvas. The black iris, or water iris, was a more exotic flower than the more common ones she usually painted. O'Keeffe may have been attracted by the iris's relatively simple structure. She painted several different examples of the flower.

The colors in all of her black iris paintings are lush and beautiful, ranging from deep black-purple and maroon to soft pink, gray, and an ivory white. All of O'Keeffe's black iris paintings are remarkably tactile. Some viewers have felt they want to reach out and feel the texture of the petals.

The shapes in this painting are reminiscent of many of the shapes O'Keeffe painted in her earlier abstract paintings. For instance, from the left side of the painting, a large, whitish gray petal shape moves

O'Keeffe painted the exotic black iris.

down the middle of the painting in much the same way as the stripe shape in *Red & Orange Streak* from 1919. Other various folds of the petals and forms of the flower also repeat many of the shapes found in her other abstract paintings. The flower provides a basic structure around which O'Keeffe composes an abstract exploration of compelling shapes and forms.

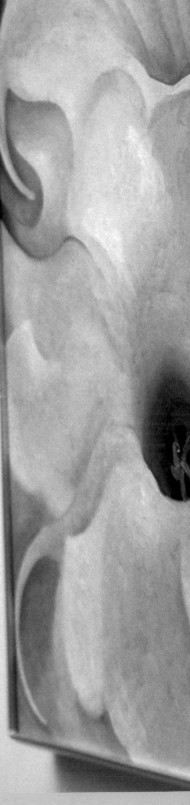

Essential Critiques

A woman viewing O'Keeffe's *Bella Donna* at an exhibition

How to Apply Feminist Criticism to *The Black Iris*

What Is Feminist Criticism?

Feminist criticism is one method that can be used to interpret art. Throughout history, men have mostly controlled the production of art and how it is received. Feminists assert it is important to take into account the female viewpoint in art. Feminist critics think about the roles gender and female sexuality play in the work of art.

One key notion of feminist criticism is that men and women have different life experiences and might approach the world differently. Women may also approach art in different ways than men do. This does not mean art by women is worse, or better, than art by men. It is just different. And feminist critics believe these different artistic approaches should be equally valued.

Applying Feminist Criticism to *The Black Iris*

In *The Black Iris,* O'Keeffe shows her unique approach to painting flowers. Unlike traditional flower painters throughout history, she painted flowers as abstract and mysterious objects. She achieved this by focusing close-up on the flower forms, simplifying the shapes, and filling her canvas with vivid brushstrokes and colors. O'Keeffe painted flowers from such a close view that they do not look much like flowers any more. The abstract form of the flower in *The Black Iris* hints at female physicality and promotes female bodies as both powerful and beautiful.

Because O'Keeffe abstracts the shapes and lines of the iris flower in *The Black Iris,* it is difficult to tell exactly what is being depicted. At first glance, it seems clear *The Black Iris* depicts a flower. And after all, the painting was strongly influenced by real flowers

---

Thesis Statement

The thesis statement in this critique is: "The abstract form of the flower in *The Black Iris* hints at female physicality and promotes female bodies as both powerful and beautiful." This thesis addresses the question: How does *The Black Iris* relate to women?

Argument One

The author has started to argue his thesis. The author sets up the full argument by first noting that the elements of the painting make its subject mysterious: "Because O'Keeffe abstracts the shapes and lines of the iris flower in *The Black Iris,* it is difficult to tell exactly what is being depicted."

O'Keeffe observed. Many of the shapes in the painting look natural and believable as parts of a flower. The paint was applied in imperceptible brushstrokes. This gives a velvety look to the flower petals, which is just how they look in nature.

However, *The Black Iris* is not a realistic depiction of a flower. Some of the shapes in *The Black Iris* do not represent anything a viewer would see when looking at a real iris flower. For example, a squiggly black shape runs from the middle circle to the bottom of the image. Also, to the right of the black squiggle, white and gray wavy shapes fill the space. These shapes would not appear on the actual flower as seen in nature. This makes it harder to tell exactly what the painting depicts.

Additionally, only the petals and center of the flower are shown in this painting. There is no stem or leaf. This makes it less evident that the painting actually depicts a flower. Without the title, *The Black Iris,* would a viewer recognize the flower in the painting?

The Black Iris seems to represent female genitalia. Some

> **Argument Two**
> The author focuses on the first part of the thesis that claims *The Black Iris* depicts the female body: "The Black Iris seems to represent female genitalia." The author will back up this claim with evidence from the painting.

of the shapes and textures in the painting might remind the viewer of the sexual parts of a woman's body. In the center of *The Black Iris,* for example, a dark, reddish circle seems to suggest a hole, which could represent a woman's vagina. Around this hole, ruffled shapes of white, bluish gray, and grayish pink may suggest forms that could be folds of skin such as those in a woman's genital area. The velvet look of the petals seems to represent a similar texture to that of human skin.

Argument Three

In this point, the author is setting up a new argument to prove the second part of the thesis that asserts that this painting promotes the female body. The author focuses on the ambiguity of the subject: "Because it is difficult to tell what exactly is being depicted in the painting, *The Black Iris* demands the attention of its viewers."

Because it is difficult to tell what exactly is being depicted in the painting, *The Black Iris* demands the attention of its viewers. Viewers might first assume they are simply looking at a flower painting. However, when they realize the painting does not look exactly like flowers they have seen in nature, they might consider other possibilities. The viewers may look at the painting for a long time, trying to figure out what they are seeing. The mystery over what they are seeing demands they pay extra attention to the painting.

O'Keeffe's *Red Poppy No. VI*, 1928

The mysterious nature of the painting paired with its similarity to female genitalia promotes the female body as a powerful thing because it demands the viewer's attention. Viewers may gaze at this painting for a long time. They may appreciate the different shapes and brush strokes. Since the painting so closely resembles female genitalia, it is valid to say viewers would also be appreciating the female body by appreciating this painting. And so, the female body, as it is depicted in *The Black Iris*, becomes something that is worthy of attention.

Argument Four

The author is tying up the loose ends of his thesis statement with the claim: "The mysterious nature of the painting paired with its similarity to female genitalia promotes the female body as a powerful thing because it demands the viewer's attention."

Argument Five

Now, the author ties up the last part of the thesis that all of the arguments have been leading to. He claims: "Furthermore, because *The Black Iris* depicts both a beautiful flower and female genitalia, it promotes the female body, specifically female sexual parts, as beautiful."

Furthermore, because <u>*The Black Iris* depicts both a beautiful flower and female genitalia, it promotes the female body, specifically female sexual parts, as beautiful.</u> Flowers are generally considered to be a beautiful part of the natural world. People display them in their homes and send them to each other for special occasions. Flowers are also often considered feminine objects. Because this painting seems to represent both a flower and genitalia at the same time, female genitalia take on the properties of a beautiful flower. Therefore, the female body becomes as beautiful as a flower.

The abstract forms of *The Black Iris* depict both a flower and female physicality. These depictions and the debate over what exactly is being depicted promote the female body as beautiful and powerful because of the attention the painting demands. Overall, *The Black Iris* promotes women's bodies as both beautiful and powerful.

Conclusion

The last paragraph of the critique sums up the author's argument. It explains again what the author has argued and proven in this essay.

Thinking Critically about *The Black Iris*

Now it's your turn to assess the critique.
Consider these questions:

1. The thesis argues *The Black Iris* promotes women's bodies as beautiful and powerful. Do you agree? Why or why not?

2. How does this argument relate to your life? Why do you think it would be important to promote women's bodies as beautiful and powerful?

3. Do you think the author missed any important points? If so, what are they?

4. What other claims might you make about the femininity of this work?

Other Approaches

You have just finished reading one author's way of applying feminist criticism to *The Black Iris*. Remember that feminist criticism focuses on how women are represented in a work. How have other experts approached this topic? Two alternate approaches follow. One focuses on how some of the same claims made by the author in this critique could lead others to assert *The Black Iris* cannot be compared to great works created by famous male artists during O'Keeffe's time. The other pertains to how O'Keeffe's work was originally promoted as sexualized and specifically female.

The Backlash of Presenting Female Issues

Some critics have claimed that because O'Keeffe's work focuses on things that were stereotypically feminine or paintings that may depict the female body, her work was less appreciated and not taken seriously as art. So, rather than presenting women and their bodies as worthy of attention, the work pigeonholes O'Keeffe as a female artist, dealing with only female concerns. Such a label takes away attention from O'Keeffe's real value as an artist and how she might match up against the male artists of her time.

The thesis statement of this claim would be:
The apparent display of female physicality in O'Keeffe's work, such as *The Black Iris*, promotes female artists as more valuable for their expression of the female experience than their talent as artists alongside men.

O'Keeffe's Work Was Marketed with a Focus on Female Sexuality

It has been suggested by some scholars that O'Keeffe's husband, Alfred Stieglitz, was the first to interpret works such as *The Black Iris* as depictions of the female body. Many believe people saw O'Keeffe's art as sexual images because Stieglitz worked to market it as such. He took photographs of O'Keeffe posing nude in front of many of her paintings.

The thesis statement of this claim would be:
O'Keeffe's work was seen as focusing on female issues and sexuality because of the way it was marketed.

Red Hills with White Shell, 1938

Chapter

7

An Overview of
Red Hills with White Shell

The paintings O'Keeffe made in New
Mexico are marked by their wide-open
quality and the brightness of the light
she depicted. In 1929, during her first
summer in New Mexico, O'Keeffe was
surprised there were so few flowers.
The region was mostly high desert
with little rain to nourish many plant
species.

During her second summer in New Mexico,
however, O'Keeffe became fascinated with the
bones she found on hikes and drives through the
desert. She began collecting the bones, which
eventually found their way into her paintings. As
with the flower paintings of the 1920s, O'Keeffe
tended to abstract the forms, shapes, and colors she

saw, even as she carefully observed real places to paint them. She recorded both a clear sense of what the landscape looked like and a strong expressive sense of how it felt to be in these places.

Over time, O'Keeffe's fascination with the colors she found in the desert landscape increased. In addition to the blue of the sky, she loved the deep reds, purples, browns, and blacks she saw in the hillsides as the light changed throughout the day. She was drawn to the bleached-white and gray quality of certain hills and of the bones she found. She once wrote,

> It is surprising to me to see how many people separate the objective from the abstract. Objective painting is not good painting unless it is good in the abstract sense. A hill or tree cannot make a good painting just because it is a hill or a tree. It is lines and colors put together so that they say something. For me that is the very basis of painting. The abstraction is often the most definite form for the intangible thing in myself that I can only clarify in paint.[1]

Red Hills with White Shell

O'Keeffe created her painting titled *Red Hills with White Shell* in 1938—only a few years after she discovered Ghost Ranch, outside Abiquiu, New Mexico. It is an oil painting on a 30 x 36 1/4 in. (76 x 93 cm) canvas. The key feature of the painting is a large white shell that fills the central portion of the painting. The shell is vastly oversized in comparison to the bright red hills, the sliver of yellow sky, and the equally bright red clouds that fill the background of the painting.

Red Hills with White Shell is overall a strange, mixed-up vision. In the middle of the painting, situated like a bull's-eye, O'Keeffe painted a large shell. Its soft white, pink, and yellow colors and swirling vortex shape are lovely to look at. But the form looks odd—much too large, against the background of a large, fiery red hill painted in a somewhat abstract and expressive fashion. The bright red hill, with its rivulets and valleys that look like waves, forces the viewer's eye upward, to a small expanse of sky. And the sky is strangely colored bright yellow. Bright red cloudlike shapes drift above the yellow sky.

The Shell

One of the more interesting features of *Red Hills with White Shell* is the close attention O'Keeffe paid to the shell. Not only does the shape dominate the painting, but the shell is painted with great care. In particular, O'Keeffe focuses on the details of the spiral form of the shell. The spiral starts from a large opening and then moves in an ever-tightening spiral until it disappears.

In addition, O'Keeffe plays with the color of the mostly white shell so that it resembles a more colorful object. In the shell, O'Keeffe includes bluish gray, pink, light yellow, and ochre. The dull white is transformed into something much more colorful than it likely was.

The Red Hills

Contrasting to the shell, the red hills in the background are vast swaths of fiery and abstract color. Bright vermillion and scarlet reds, hot pinks, flame orange, and burgundy shapes meld together to create the one great hill behind the large shell. In scale, the hill seems, especially when compared to the massive foreground shell, much smaller than real life. In terms of color, the hills are much

brighter, more vibrant and alive, than they would appear in nature.

The landscape in Abiquiu, New Mexico, inspired O'Keeffe.

The Sky

The sky too is an unrealistic element in *Red Hills with White Shell*. Painted in layers of dull pink, bright yellow, and bluish gray before giving way to a cover of bright red clouds, this sky is imaginative. The clouds are overly bright and redder than any real cloud. O'Keeffe must have had much more in mind than depicting a simple sunset fading over red hills.

O'Keeffe painted *Red White and Blue* in 1931.

How to Apply Biographical Criticism to *Red Hills with White Shell*

What Is Biographical Criticism?

Biographical criticism is a method for critiquing art that takes into account details from the artist's life. In this method, the critic is interested in seeking connections between biographical information about the artist and the work of art. How the critic interprets the meanings of the art is then based on an understanding of the context of the artist's life experiences.

When critiquing art through the lens of biographical criticism, the artist's life must be researched for major events or recurring patterns that may have influenced the artist's work. Knowing the story of an artist's life can give clues to the meaning behind certain works of art. One must keep in mind, however, that making a work of art is not the same as telling one's life story. Making art is an act of creation, so often biographic details only indirectly influence what an artist paints or sculpts. With a bit of detective work, however, interesting connections may be made between a work of art and the life of the artist who made it.

Applying Biographical Criticism to *Red Hills with White Shell*

From an early age, O'Keeffe lived the life of a traveler. She was born in the Midwest and moved to Virginia while in high school. As an adult, she lived in many different places, including Illinois, Texas, New York, and New Mexico. Hardly a year went by that she did not travel across the North American continent. Considering her lifetime of travel, it would make sense that O'Keeffe's art would reflect a unique outlook on new places. Indeed, O'Keeffe's painting *Red Hills with White Shell* reveals her sharp connection to the land and her endless curiosity about exotic new places.

Thesis Statement

The thesis statement in this critique is: "O'Keeffe's painting *Red Hills with White Shell* reveals her sharp connection to the land and her endless curiosity about exotic new places." This thesis addresses the questions: What does *Red Hills with White Shell* reveal about O'Keeffe's life? How did O'Keeffe's experiences influence her painting *Red Hills with White Shell*?

With *Red Hills with White Shell*, O'Keeffe depicts a harsh and dry land with tenderness and appreciation. *Red Hills with White Shell* evokes the look of the wide American desert of the Southwest. This area is often thought of as a dry, rugged, and harsh land. It can be extremely hot. It can be a difficult place to live because of the heat and dry air. However, *Red Hills with White Shell* does not depict the Southwest in these negative terms. Rather, the painting reveals the appreciation O'Keeffe had for the American desert. To O'Keeffe, connection with the landscape was always very important. She was quoted as saying, "It is necessary to feel America, like America, love America, and then work."[1]

In the strange beauty of the bright and fiery hills and sky she painted in *Red Hills with White Shell*, it is clear O'Keeffe explored a landscape she deeply appreciated. The colors seem to come out of a religious painting—bright, otherworldly, and meant to be worshipped. The way she painted the shell,

> **Argument One**
>
> The author has started to argue his thesis. This is his first point: "With *Red Hills with White Shell*, O'Keeffe depicts a harsh and dry land with tenderness and appreciation." This point focuses on proving how O'Keeffe felt about the painting she created and how it relates to the landscape that served as her model.

and this desert landscape, is full of reverence and love. The hills resemble a velvet, red bedcover that is tactile and warm. The shell resembles a newborn infant, flush with life and resting against the warm bed of the desert. It is clear O'Keeffe worshipped the beauty and life of the American desert.

O'Keeffe's *Red Hills with White Shell* reveals her fondness for exploration. Throughout her life, O'Keeffe was dedicated to constantly seeing new sights and doing new things. She counted on her life experiences and observations to influence her art. She once said, "Where I was born and where and how I have lived is unimportant. It is what I have done with where I have been that should be of interest."[2]

O'Keeffe interacted with the landscapes she saw during her long life in several ways. She interacted visually with the landscape through her art. Throughout her life, she moved through the landscape and experienced it during her long walks and car and train rides across the land. She experienced the land sensually by feeling the wind,

> **Argument Two**
> The author expands on his point about the scene O'Keeffe painted. He adds to his claim by asserting: "O'Keeffe's *Red Hills with White Shell* reveals her fondness for exploration."

In *Red Hills with White Shell*, O'Keeffe painted the shell with great care.

soil, plants, and rocks. O'Keeffe related to the landscape by dedicating her life to painting it.

Above all else, *Red Hills with White Shell,* with its vibrant hills and fiery, open skies, reveals O'Keeffe's appreciation of being free to move and travel. The energy of this image, and its warmth and beauty, evokes the ancient beauty of the land and the appeal of new and interesting spaces. The painting's colors and energy hint at O'Keeffe's

Argument Three

In his next point, the author narrows his argument by suggesting what exactly it was about travel that was so appealing to O'Keeffe and how it is shown in the painting. He claims: "Above all else, *Red Hills with White Shell,* with its vibrant hills and fiery, open skies, reveals O'Keeffe's appreciation of being free to move and travel."

own appreciation of the vast landscapes she had experienced in her own life. The colors are bright, exciting yellows that stir up the emotions O'Keeffe likely felt when exploring a new place. Beyond the yellow sky and the horizon behind the red hills, the Southwest desert and the rest of the open country seem to beckon to the viewer.

Still, that leaves a question as to why O'Keeffe chose to focus so closely on the large shell shape that fills much of her desert image. It is likely the shell relates to the particular appreciation of the American landscape that O'Keeffe developed from her travels. The shells in O'Keeffe's paintings from this era are found throughout the Southwest desert. They are remnants of an ancient sea that once covered this land. "Each shell is a beautiful world in itself," O'Keeffe said about her interest in the objects.[3]

To O'Keeffe, desert shells were both exotic and familiar. They were new and unusual objects, unexpected in the dry and arid conditions of the Southwest. Much as a traveler looks for souvenirs of places visited, O'Keeffe studied these shells. She painted them reverently, like relics of a foreign land. At the same time, she thought they were evocative

of the seas she had known and loved. <u>In *Red Hills*</u> <u>*with White Shell*, O'Keeffe paints the desert both</u> <u>as an exotic and new sight, as well as a majestic</u>

O'Keeffe even enjoyed exploring her own backyard.

Argument Four

The author has arrived at his final point. He relies on information about O'Keeffe's travels throughout her life to claim how such places affected her art. He claims: "In *Red Hills with White Shell*, O'Keeffe paints the desert both as an exotic and new sight, as well as a majestic and beautifully familiar one, the ocean."

Conclusion

This final paragraph is the conclusion of the critique. It sums up the author's arguments and partially restates the original thesis, which has now been argued and supported with evidence. The author also ponders the oddity of O'Keeffe including both the familiar scenes from her life and exploring new exotic ones in a single painting.

and beautifully familiar one, the ocean.

This blending of O'Keeffe's interests in the land creates much of the power and appeal of *Red Hills with White Shell*. In an appealing composition, she painted the exotic new landscapes she discovered throughout her life. At the same time, she hints at her enduring love for the comforts of ocean views she had appreciated in her younger years. It may seem strange that O'Keeffe's paintings can evoke the familiar even as she explores the exotic—but this reflects her life as a curious traveler who adored her home.

Thinking Critically about *Red Hills with White Shell*

Now it's your turn to assess the critique.
Consider these questions:

1. The thesis focuses on how *Red Hills with White Shell* displays O'Keeffe's love of travel and exploration. Do you agree the work asserts this idea? Why or why not?

2. Do you think O'Keeffe meant to show her appreciation for travel with this painting? Why else might she have created this painting? What other biographical ties can you make between O'Keeffe's life and *Red Hills with White Shell*?

3. What was the best argument made in the critique? Why do you like it? Is there anything you would add to that argument? What was the weakest argument? Why did it not convince you?

Other Approaches

You have just read one author's application of biographical criticism to *Red Hills with White Shell*. What are some other ways experts have approached it? Remember that biographical criticism looks at how an artist's work was inspired by personal life events. Two alternate approaches follow. The first claims O'Keeffe is a feminist artist. The second examines the effect O'Keeffe's marriage to Alfred Stieglitz may have had on this painting.

O'Keeffe's Artwork Reflected Her Life as a Feminist

Although O'Keeffe strongly denied any of her work had feminist intentions, many scholars continue to point to her as a premier feminist artist. Critic Jillian P. Cowley asserts, "O'Keeffe was one of a number of women artists during this period who, through both their lifestyles and their images, helped expand the range of what was possible and accepted for women. Her strong portrayals of the harsh and vast desert landscape moved the norm for women artists' subject matter even further from the earlier norm of small-scale nature and domestic scenes."[4]

The thesis statement for a critique that examines O'Keeffe's art as feminist might be: O'Keeffe's depiction of harsh desert landscapes as in *Red Hills with White Shell* reveals her push to break out of the artistic conventions held for female artists of her time.

The Painting Reflects O'Keeffe's Relationship with Her Husband

Many O'Keeffe scholars have studied the relationship between O'Keeffe and her husband, Alfred Stieglitz, who was more than 20 years her senior. In addition to the disparity in their ages, there were many other differences between the two artists. He focused on photography; she preferred painting. He enjoyed New York and never traveled to the West and the land that O'Keeffe adored. One might suspect this painting pairs the seemingly unrelated "white shell" with "red hills," just as O'Keeffe and Stieglitz were paired in their marriage.

The thesis statement for this critique might be: The ironic pairing of a seashell with a desert scene in *Red Hills with White Shell* reveals O'Keeffe's feelings about her unconventional marriage to Alfred Stieglitz.

O'Keeffe standing in front of *Pelvis Series Red with Yellow*

An Overview of *Pelvis Series Red with Yellow*

A spectrum of yellows, from mustard
to lemon, fills a large ovular space in
the center of O'Keeffe's rectangular
composition *Pelvis Series Red with
Yellow* from 1945. This bright yellow
imperfectly shaped oval is surrounded
by various hues of red. Fiery reds
predominate in the space surrounding
the central, yellow oval.

But in the bottom right corner of the canvas, the
intense reds fade to flesh tones. In the upper right
corner of the canvas, O'Keeffe included a white
highlight. The red that surrounds the yellow oval
shape appears almost liquid, and O'Keeffe's use of
line in the upper right corner gives the composition
a sense of flow and movement.

This oil on canvas painting is 36 x 48 in. (91.4 x 121.9 cm) and horizontally oriented. It is part of a series of paintings of animal pelvic bones that O'Keeffe began during the 1930s and early 1940s. If not for the title, one might not associate this work with an animal pelvis, because the scale and use of color are abstract. We do not think of bones as bright red, and we do not imagine the hollow voids of bones to appear bright yellow. Upon realizing that O'Keeffe depicts a vastly magnified bone and empty space, it becomes clear that this work is both an abstract impression and a representation of a real object and landscape.

Painting Bones

At an exhibition in January 1944, a year before she finished *Pelvis Series Red with Yellow*, O'Keeffe unveiled her new series of paintings in which she used animal pelvic bones as framing devices. Just as we place photographs in frames, O'Keeffe uses the bony structure of the pelvis to frame the hollow space it surrounds. Like human and animal skulls that have holes where the eyes and nose were once attached, pelvic bones have holes where legs were once attached.

It is these holes, rather than the bone itself, that O'Keeffe focused upon in her pelvic series. O'Keeffe explained, "[W]hen I started painting the pelvis bones I was most interested in the holes of the bones—what I saw through them—particularly the blue from holding them up in the sun against the sky as one is apt to do when one seems to have more sky than earth in one's world."[1] In earlier paintings of the series, such as *Pelvis I (Pelvis*

O'Keeffe collected animal bones and antlers while living in New Mexico.

with Blue) from 1944, O'Keeffe used blue paint to represent the sky peeking through the white bone's circular hollow. It was not until *Pelvis Series Red with Yellow* that she began to experiment with abstract colors in the pelvic series.

The color palette of her earlier work, *Pelvis I*, is representational of the actual bone and sky on which O'Keeffe based her interpretation. In *Pelvis Series Red with Yellow,* O'Keeffe used colors more abstractly. However, the two works have a very similar arrangement of shapes. Both works have dominant oval voids at their centers surrounded by a carefully shaded contrasting color. In both works, O'Keeffe played with relative size and scale, exaggerating the size of the empty hole relative to the bone that surrounds it.

While we might tend to focus our attention on objects rather than the space around and between those objects, O'Keeffe redirects our eye to the negative space we typically overlook. She makes the empty void the subject of this painting, rather than the solid pelvic bone. O'Keeffe radically simplifies the shapes of the composition to a circular solid-and-void and the colors of the composition to intense yellow, red, and white.

The New Mexico Landscape

Bones are powerful symbols of the rural Southwest and often appear in the works O'Keeffe painted in New Mexico—where she settled late in her life. O'Keeffe was taken in by the wide expanses of land, the bright blue skies that extended infinitely in every direction, and the relative isolation of New Mexico life. While O'Keeffe used less obvious colors in *Pelvis Series Red with Yellow* than in *Pelvis I*, both were inspired by the New Mexico landscape and the unusually vibrant sunsets of the New Mexico sky. We can imagine how, if the sun caught the surface of the bone in a particular way, it might have given O'Keeffe the impression of a bright red bone against a bright yellow sky, which inspired her strikingly beautiful impression of this moment in *Pelvis Series Red with Yellow*.

Deer's Skull with Pedernal, 1936

How to Apply Structuralism to
Pelvis Series Red with Yellow

What Is Structuralism?

Structuralism was an influential intellectual movement of the twentieth century that sought to consider and theorize the relationship between language and meaning. Effectively, structuralists suggest that language does not merely convey meaning, but that it produces meaning. This sounds like a very complicated idea, but it is really quite simple when broken down.

Imagine that while riding in a car you see a road sign with a yellow *M* on the side of the highway. Most Americans, and increasingly most people from around the world, would recognize this ever-present symbol as representing a McDonald's restaurant chain. The yellow letter *M* has not always been a signifier of McDonald's. The relationship between this symbol and the restaurant does not occur naturally. To understand this idea more clearly, imagine a time before McDonald's existed when the *M* symbol and the name *McDonald's* would not have meant anything to Americans. It was marketers who promoted the *M* symbol, and our society started to recognize the yellow *M* as representing the fast-food restaurant chain. In other words, this relationship is culturally constructed by means of social arrangements and rules. All words and symbols had to be invented and assigned meaning through usage. An underlying structure makes meaning possible.

When we apply structuralism to art, we do not understand the artist as producing the meaning of the work. Instead, we understand the artist selects signs with socially determined meanings and combines them to communicate something specific. Viewers analyze the work to suggest what the combination of shapes, objects, and symbols conveys. The conditions under which a work of art was made and the artist's intentions are irrelevant to a structuralist analysis. Structuralists analyze works of art as socially meaningful visual systems to be decoded.

Applying Structuralism to *Pelvis Series Red with Yellow*

In O'Keeffe's *Pelvis Series Red with Yellow*, the central signifier to decode is the dominant void or egg-shaped sphere at the center of the composition. While it makes reference to itself, the oval shape, it also gestures toward concepts such as wholeness and infinity. There is a symbolic relationship between the bright yellow oval and the red space that surrounds it, which depends not only upon the symbolic meaning of the separate elements but also upon the symbolic relationship between these elements. The spherical space at the center of the composition represents not only a circle; it also represents a hole or cavity in the bone through which the viewer is made to look. The yellow cavity represents the sky, which is surrounded by red bone. The bone seems to represent Earth and mortality; the sky represents the heavens. *Pelvis Series Red with Yellow* displays the fragility of a moral life and a spiritual afterlife and a separation between the two.

> **Thesis Statement**
>
> The thesis statement in this critique is: "*Pelvis Series Red with Yellow* displays the fragility of a moral life and a spiritual afterlife and a separation between the two." This thesis addresses the questions: What symbols are present in *Pelvis Series Red with Yellow*? And what do they represent?

Within structuralism, a circle is understandable by virtue of the fact that it is not a square or a triangle. Like all other signs, it operates according to a system of differences. Signs often operate as pairs, couplings, and oppositions. Black is understandable in opposition to white, culture in opposition to nature, female in opposition to male, and active in opposition to passive. The spherical space at the center of the composition represents not only a circle, but also a hole or cavity in the bone.

The yellow spherical space at the center of the composition represents a hole or cavity in the bone, but also displays the sky and relates to the heavens and creation. Many have suggested that the spherical form is a socially constructed signifier of the ancient symbol of creation. Because of this, the egg-shaped circle in *Pelvis Series Red with Yellow* may be seen as a symbol for creation and life cycles.

The yellow circle also seems to depict the sky through a hole in the red bone. However, sky is

> **Argument One**
>
> The author has started to argue his thesis. This is his first point: "The yellow spherical space at the center of the composition represents a hole or cavity in the bone, but also displays the sky and relates to the heavens and creation." In this point, the author is focusing on the yellow egg-shaped circle in the center of the painting and what it might represent.

usually thought of as blue in color. In several other pelvic paintings, O'Keeffe depicted the sky as blue and the bones as white.

O'Keeffe standing next to some of her paintings in 1970

So, the bright yellow tone used in *Pelvis Series Red with Yellow* may represent something other than sky. Because it is yellow, it may be perceived as sunlight streaming in through the bone. The color yellow may also signify a divine or heavenly light. As early as the Renaissance, painters depicted the sky as a way of referencing the celestial heavens. So, the sky in *Pelvis Series Red with Yellow* may represent a spiritual power or experience. The sky does not inherently or naturally have associations with God, the heavens, and spirituality, but this symbolic relationship comes into play in this painting.

Argument Two

The author has now shifted focus to discuss the red bone in the painting: "The pelvic bone in this painting represents mortality." The author is proving the part of his thesis that asserts that the painting focuses on mortality.

The pelvic bone in this painting represents mortality. Bones, as symbols, are linked to death. After all, bones separated from a body often means that whatever the bone belonged to has died and decayed. In the history of Western art, artists have painted skulls in their compositions to serve as memento mori. This Latin phrase means, "remember that you must die." Painters included skulls in their paintings as a reminder to the viewer that everyone will eventually die. The red bone in this painting serves to remind the viewer of death.

The fact that the bone is colored rather than white also works to represent mortality. The color of the bone disrupts the natural appearance of a bone. Red typically signifies bravery, happiness, heat, energy, blood, anger, passion, love, pain, and sacrifice. Undoubtedly, it does not often signify all of these characteristics at once. In this painting, the red is a reminder of the energy and life that once applied to the bone when the animal was alive. It also relates to the pain, and perhaps violence, that comes with death.

> **Argument Three**
>
> In this point, the author continues to explore the symbolism of the red bone. Now, he is focusing on the color of the bone. "The fact that the bone is colored rather than white also works to represent mortality."

The red bone appears as a barrier between itself and the bright yellow shape in the middle of the painting. The placement of the bone brings to mind the barrier between a mortal world and a divine heaven. The very clear separation of the red and the yellow along this line work to further create a barrier between these worlds. The mortal world and the divine world are firmly separated.

> **Argument Four**
>
> The author centers on the final point of his thesis by claiming: "The placement of the bone brings to mind the barrier between a mortal world and a divine heaven."

O'Keeffe at 80 years old

Neither O'Keeffe nor the viewer invents the meaning of *Pelvis Series Red with Yellow.* It is instead something that is made possible by an arbitrary system of relationships, upon which all members of society agree. In O'Keeffe's *Pelvis Series Red with Yellow*, she arranged predetermined cultural symbols of bone, sky, and color to gesture toward the mysterious relationship between life and death.

Conclusion

This final paragraph is the conclusion of the critique. It sums up the author's arguments and partially restates the original thesis, which has now been argued and supported with evidence.

Thinking Critically about *Pelvis Series Red with Yellow*

Now it's your turn to assess the critique.

Consider these questions:

1. The thesis asserts that the painting depicts Earth and heaven and the barrier between the two. Do you see this in the painting?

2. The author argues that the bone represents death and the yellow oval represents the afterlife. Do you agree? Why or why not? What do you think they represent?

3. Structuralism focuses on the use of symbols that create meaning. Do you see any other symbols in the painting? If so, what? What meanings might these other symbols have?

Other Approaches

What you have just read is just one possible way to apply structuralism to this painting. What are some other ways experts have approached it? Remember that structuralism focuses on symbols that are predefined in our society. Two alternate approaches follow. The first focuses on the color in the painting. The second asserts that the painting represents a life cycle.

The Painting Represents the Heat of the Desert Landscape

One way to look at *Pelvis Series Red with Yellow* from a structuralist standpoint is to look solely at what the colors represent. The warm reds and yellows O'Keeffe used in this painting seem to depict a very warm or hot climate. For example, these colors might symbolize a desert scene.

A thesis statement for this observation might be: The warm reds and yellows used in *Pelvis Series Red with Yellow* evoke a hot desert.

The Painting Represents the Earthly Life Cycle

Another way one might view *Pelvis Series Red with Yellow* is to view the yellow oval shape in the center of the painting as the yoke of an egg. One could assert that because the painting displays an egg in the center and a bone surrounding it, it depicts life in both an unborn (egg) state and a dead (bone) one.

A thesis statement for this argument might be: *Pelvis Series Red with Yellow* displays a life moving from an embryonic state to a deceased one.

You Critique It

Now that you have learned about several different critical theories and how to apply them to art, are you ready to perform a critique of your own? You have read that this type of evaluation can help you look at art from a new perspective and make you pay attention to certain issues you may not have otherwise recognized. So, why not use one of the critical theories profiled in this book to consider a fresh take on your favorite work?

First, choose a theory and the artwork you want to analyze. Remember that the theory is a springboard for asking questions about the work.

Next, write a specific question that relates to the theory you have selected. Then you can form your thesis, which should provide the answer to that question. Your thesis is the most important part of your critique and offers an argument about the work based on the tenets, or beliefs, of the theory you are applying. Recall that the thesis statement typically appears at the very end of the introductory paragraph of your essay. It is usually only one sentence long.

After you have written your thesis, find evidence to back it up. Good places to start are in the work itself or journals or articles that discuss what other people have said about it. Since you are critiquing a work of art, you may also want to read about the artist's life to get a sense of what factors may have affected the creative process. This can be especially useful if working within historical, biographical, or psychological criticism.

Depending on which theory you apply, you can often find evidence in the art's subject, its color and form, or the artist's technique. You should also explore aspects of the work that seem to disprove your thesis and create an argument against them. As you do this, you might want to address what other critics have written about the artwork. Their quotes may help support your claim.

Before you start analyzing a work, think about the different arguments made in this book. Reflect on how evidence supporting the thesis was presented. Did you find that some of the techniques used to back up the arguments were more convincing than others? Try these methods as you prove your thesis in your own critique.

When you are finished writing your critique, read it over carefully. Is your thesis statement understandable? Do the supporting arguments flow logically, with the topic of each paragraph clearly stated? Can you add any information that would present your readers with a stronger argument in favor of your thesis? Were you able to use evidence from the artwork as well as quotes from critics to enhance your ideas?

Did you see the work in a new light?

Timeline

O'Keeffe attends the School of the Art Institute of Chicago.

1907–1908

O'Keeffe attends the Art Students League of New York.

1908

O'Keeffe is awarded the league's Still Life Scholarship in June.

1887

Georgia Totto O'Keeffe is born near Sun Prairie, Wisconsin, on November 15.

1946

Stieglitz is found unconscious from a stroke on July 10. O'Keeffe returns to New York City from New Mexico.

Stieglitz dies on July 13.

1949

O'Keeffe settles permanently in New Mexico in June.

1962

O'Keeffe is elected to the 50-member American Academy of Arts and Letters.

1916 In the summer, O'Keeffe moves to Canyon, Texas, to teach. Alfred Stieglitz includes O'Keeffe's work in a group show at 291 Gallery.

1917 Stieglitz opens Georgia O'Keeffe, the first one-person show of her work, at 291 Gallery on April 3.

1918 O'Keeffe moves to New York City on June 10.

1923 Stieglitz opens the show titled Alfred Stieglitz Presents One Hundred Pictures: Oils, Water-colors, Pastels, Drawings, by Georgia O'Keeffe, American on January 29.

1924 O'Keeffe and Stieglitz marry on December 11.

1925–1933 Stieglitz mounts a series of solo exhibitions of O'Keeffe's work at various galleries.

1940 O'Keeffe purchases a house on Ghost Ranch in New Mexico.

1970 O'Keeffe's retrospective occurs at the Whitney Museum of American Art in October.

1977 O'Keeffe is awarded the Presidential Medal of Freedom by Gerald Ford.

1986 O'Keeffe dies in Santa Fe, New Mexico, on March 6.

Glossary

abstract art
> Art that does not refer to real visual references and, instead, attempts to depict spiritual and emotional truths common to humans.

art critic
> A professional writer of art criticism.

avant-garde
> A cultural attempt in the arts to push the boundaries of what is accepted as the norm.

composition
> The placement or arrangement of visual elements in a work of art.

illusionistic
> Made to resemble objects as they appear in real life.

landscape
> Art that depicts scenery such as mountains, valleys, trees, rivers, and forests.

modernism
> Experimental art forms of the early twentieth century. Various twentieth-century art movements are included in the umbrella term modernism.

negative space
> Empty space in a work of art.

objective
> Not affected by personal opinion.

representational
> Meant to depict something real.

retrospective
> An art exhibit showing representative examples of
> an artist's lifework.

still life
> A work of art depicting mostly inanimate subjects
> set in an artificial setting.

tactile
> Perceptible to the sense of touch. In painting, it
> refers to objects that seem so real that it seems like
> you could reach out and feel them.

Bibliography of Works and Criticism

Important Works

Evening Star No. V, 1917 (Watercolor on paper, 9" x 12")

Light Coming on the Plains III, 1917 (Watercolor on paper, 12" x 8")

Music, Pink and Blue No. 2, 1919 (Oil on canvas, 35" x 29 1/8")

A Storm, 1922 (Pastel on paper, mounted on illustration board, 18 1/4" x 24 3/8")

Red Canna, 1923 (Oil on canvas, 36" x 30")

Flower Abstraction, 1924 (Oil on canvas, 48" x 30")

The Black Iris, 1926 (Oil on canvas, 9" x 7")

Line and Curve, 1927 (Oil on canvas, 31 15/16" x 16 1/4")

Oriental Poppies, 1927 (Oil on canvas, 30" x 40 1/8")

Shell No. I, 1928 (Oil on canvas, 7" x 7")

New York, Night, 1929 (Oil on canvas, 40" x 19")

Jack-in-the-Pulpit VI, 1930 (Oil on canvas, 36" x 18")

Cow's Skull: Red, White, and Blue, 1931 (Oil on canvas, 40" x 36")

The Shell, 1934 (Charcoal on laid paper, 18 5/8" x 24 1/2")

Red Hills with White Shell, 1938 (Oil on canvas, 30" x 36 1/4")

Red Hills and Bones, 1941 (Oil on canvas, 29 3/4" x 40")

Cottonwood III, 1944 (Oil on canvas, 19 1/2" x 29 1/4")

Pelvis I (Pelvis with Blue), 1944 (Oil on canvas, 36" x 30")

Pelvis Series Red with Yellow, 1945 (Oil on canvas, 36" x 48")

Poppies, 1950 (Oil on canvas, 36" x 30")

Black Door with Red, 1955 (Oil on canvas, 48" x 84")

Only One, 1959 (Oil on canvas, 36" x 30")

Sky with Flat White Cloud, 1962 (Oil on canvas, 60" x 80")

Sky Above Clouds IV, 1965 (Oil on canvas, 8' x 24')

Critical Discussions

Cotter, Holland. "In Full Flower, Before the Desert." *New York Times*. 17 Sept. 2009.

Cowley, Jillian P. "Gender, Landscape, and Art: Georgia O'Keeffe's Relationship with the Ghost Ranch Landscape." *Exploring the Boundaries of Historic Landscape Preservation*. The Alliance for Historic Landscape Preservation, 2007.

Jared, Amy. "Georgia O'Keeffe: Connected to Nature." *School Arts*. 1 Mar. 1997.

Mitchell, Marilyn Hall. *Sexist Art Criticism: Georgia O'Keeffe–A Case Study*. Chicago: The University of Chicago Press, 1978.

Mullan, Anthony P. "Georgia O'Keeffe in Washington: The Art and the Image." *Arts Magazine*. Mar. 1988.

Rose, Barbara. "The Truth About Georgia O'Keeffe." *Journal of Art*. Feb. 1990.

Resources

Selected Bibliography

Cowart, Jack, and Juan Hamilton. *Georgia O'Keeffe: Art and Letters*. Boston, MA: Little, Brown, 1987.

Drohojowska-Philp, Hunter. *Full Bloom: The Art and Life of Georgia O'Keeffe*. New York: W. W. Norton, 2004.

Lisle, Laurie. *Portrait of an Artist: A Bibliography of Georgia O'Keeffe*. New York: Seaview Books, 1980.

Messinger, Lisa Mintz. *Georgia O'Keeffe*. New York: Thames and Hudson, 1988.

Further Readings

Hubbard, Coleen. *Uniquely New Mexico*. Chicago, IL: Heinemann Library, 2004.

Rubin, Susan. *Wideness and Wonder: The Life and Art of Georgia O'Keeffe*. San Francisco, CA: Chronicle Books, 2010.

Thomson, Ruth. *Georgia O'Keeffe*. Danbury, CT: Franklin Watts, 2003.

Web Links

To learn more about critiquing the works of Georgia O'Keeffe, visit ABDO Publishing Company online at **www.abdopublishing.com**. Web sites about the works of Georgia O'Keeffe are featured on our Book Links page. These links are routinely monitored and updated to provide the most current information available.

For More Information

Georgia O'Keeffe Museum

217 Johnson Street, Santa Fe, NM 87501

505-946-1000

www.okeeffemuseum.org

The museum holds a collection of more than 1,000 pieces of art by O'Keeffe. The museum also exhibits the work of other past and current artists.

The Museum of Modern Art

11 West 53 Street, New York, NY 10019

212-708-9400

www.moma.org

The Museum of Modern Art features extensive collections of modern art, including works of Georgia O'Keeffe and many other modern artists.

Source Notes

Chapter 1. Introduction to Critiques
None.

Chapter 2. A Closer Look at Georgia O'Keeffe
1. Laurie Lisle. *Portrait of an Artist: A Bibliography of Georgia O'Keeffe*. New York: Seaview Books, 1980. 68.

2. Ibid. 359.

Chapter 3. An Overview of *Evening Star No. V*
1. Laurie Lisle. *Portrait of an Artist: A Bibliography of Georgia O'Keeffe*. New York: Seaview Books, 1980. 68.

Chapter 4. How to Apply Formalist Criticism to *Evening Star No. V*
1. Clement Greenberg. "Art." *Nation*. 15 June 1946. 727–28.

Chapter 5. An Overview of *The Black Iris*
None.

Chapter 6. How to Apply Feminist Criticism to *The Black Iris*
None.

Chapter 7. An Overview of *Red Hills with White Shell*

1. Georgia O'Keeffe. *Georgia O'Keeffe*. New York: Viking Press, 1976. 128.

Chapter 8. How to Apply Biographical Criticism to *Red Hills with White Shell*

1. Laurie Lisle. *Portrait of an Artist: A Bibliography of Georgia O'Keeffe*. New York: Seaview Books, 1980. 159.

2. Charles C. Eldredge. *Georgia O'Keeffe: American and Modern*. Fort Worth, TX: InterCultura, 1993. 17.

3. Georgia O'Keeffe. *Georgia O'Keeffe*. New York: Viking Press, 1976. 104.

4. Jillian P. Cowley. "Gender, Landscape, and Art: Georgia O'Keeffe's Relationship with the Ghost Ranch Landscape." *Exploring the Boundaries of Historic Landscape Preservation*. The Alliance for Historic Landscape Preservation, 2007. 132.

Source Notes Continued

Chapter 9. An Overview of *Pelvis Series Red with Yellow*

1. Sarah Whitaker Peters. *Becoming O'Keeffe: The Early Years*. New York: Abbeville Press, 2001. 353.

Chapter 10. How to Apply Structuralism to *Pelvis Series Red with Yellow*

None.

Index

abstraction, 29, 33, 40, 62

Albuquerque, New Mexico, 22

arguments, how to write, 11, 96–97

Art Institute of Chicago, 22

Art Students League, 14

Bement, Alon, 15–16, 29

biographical criticism,
> conclusion, 74
>
> evidence and arguments, 69–74
>
> other approaches, 76–77
>
> thesis statement, 68

Black Iris, The 45–59

Blue Rider group, 29

Braque, Georges, 29

Canyon, Texas, 16, 28

Chatham Episcopal Institute, 14

Chicago, Illinois, 14, 15, 22, 68

Composition: A Series of Exercises in Art Structure for the Use of Students and Teachers, 15

Cowley, Jillian P., 76

critical theory, definitions of, 6–9
> biographical criticism, 67–68
>
> feminist criticism, 51
>
> formalist criticism, 33–34
>
> structuralism, 85–86

Cubism, 29

Delaunay, Robert, 29

Dow, Arthur Wesley, 15–16

Europe, 23, 28–29, 30

Evening Star No. V, 26–43

evidence, how to use, 10, 96–97

Index

female sexuality, 51, 59
feminist criticism,
    conclusion, 56
    evidence and arguments, 52–56
    other approaches, 58–59
    thesis statement, 52
flower paintings, 46–59
formalist criticism,
    conclusion, 40
    evidence and arguments, 36–40
    other approaches, 42–43
    thesis statement, 36

Georgia O'Keeffe Museum, 24
Ghost Ranch, New Mexico, 22, 63
Greenberg, Clement, 43

Kandinsky, Wassily, 29, 30

Madison, Wisconsin, 14
Mann, Sarah, 13
Matisse, Henri, 29, 30
modern art, 14, 27, 28–31, 33, 34, 42, 43
Mondrian, Piet, 29
Museum of Modern Art, 22

New York, New York, 14–15, 18, 20, 21, 22, 27, 29, 43 45, 48, 77
1913 Armory Show, 29

O'Keeffe, Anita (sister), 15
O'Keeffe, Francis (father), 13
O'Keeffe, Georgia,
    art exhibitions, 19, 20, 22, 24
    awards, 14, 24
    childhood, 13–14
    education, 13–16
    marriage, 20
O'Keeffe, Ida (mother), 13

Pelvis I (Pelvis with Blue), 81–82, 83
Pelvis Series Red with Yellow, 78–95
Petunia, No. 2, 46
Picasso, Pablo, 29
Pollitzer, Anita, 18–19

questions, critical thinking, 41, 61, 79, 93

Red & Orange Streak, 45, 47, 49
Red Hills with White Shell, 61–77

Sacred Heart Academy, 14
Santa Fe, New Mexico, 22, 24
Stieglitz, Alfred, 18–20, 22, 29, 59, 77
structuralism,
        conclusion, 92
        evidence and arguments, 88–91
        other approaches, 94–95
        thesis statement, 87
Sun Prairie, Wisconsin, 13

Taos, New Mexico, 21–22
291 Gallery, 19–20

University of Virginia, 15

West Texas State Normal College, 16–17
Williamsburg, Virginia, 14

About the Author

Michael Fallon is an artist, arts writer, and nonprofit administrator based in Saint Paul, Minnesota. Fallon received a Master in Fine Arts in book arts from the University of Alabama. As a book artist, he worked with legendary figures such as Kurt Vonnegut, John Barth, Nikki Giovanni, and Robert Bly. Since 1998, Fallon has written reviews, feature articles, essays, and profiles on art for various publications. Today, Fallon is working on various writing projects and doing nonprofit work for institutions of higher education.

Photo Credits

MPI/Getty Images, cover, 3; Hedda Gjerpen/iStockphoto, cover, 33, 51, 67, 85, 99 (left); Yuriy Kaygorodov/iStockphoto, cover, 7; Brian Santa Maria/iStockphoto, cover, 13, 27, 45, 61, 79, 99 (right); Laura Gilpin/AP Images, 12; Georgia O'Keeffe at '291,' 1917, Alfred Stieglitz, platinum print, 9 1/4 x 7 1/4 inches/Gift of the Georgia O'Keeffe Foundation/Georgia O'Keeffe Museum, Santa Fe/Art Resource, New York/© 2010 Georgia O'Keeffe Museum/Artists Right Society (ARS), New York/2003.01.011/AS 474, 17; *Evening Star No. V*, 1917, Georgia O'Keeffe, Watercolor on paper, 8 5/8 x 11 5/8 in. (21.9 x 29.5 cm)/Bequest of Helen Miller Jones/© McNay Art Museum, San Antonio, Texas/Art Resource, New York/© 2010 Georgia O'Keeffe Museum / Artists Rights Society (ARS), New York, 26; John Phillips//Time Life Pictures/Getty Images, 21; John Loengard/Time & Life Pictures/Getty Images, 23; Eddy Risch/AP Images, 25, 98 (top); Bettmann/Corbis, 31; Susan Walsh/AP Images, 32; Charles Doswell III/Getty Images, 35; iStockphoto, 39; *The Black Iris*, 1926, Georgia O'Keeffe, Oil on canvas, 9 x 7 in. (22.9 x 17.8 cm)/Georgia O'Keeffe Museum, Santa Fe/Gift of The Burnett Foundation (2007.01.019)/Gerald and Kathleen Peter/Art Resource, New York/© 2010 Georgia O'Keeffe Museum/Artists Rights Society (ARS), New York, 44; Roberto A. Sanchez/iStockphoto, 47; Ivan Sazykin/iStockphoto, 49; Jeff Geissler/AP Images, 50; Eugene Hoshiko/AP Images, 55; *Red Hills with White Shell*, 1938 (oil on canvas), O'Keeffe, Georgia (1887-1986)/Museum of Fine Arts, Houston, Texas, USA/© DACS/Gift of Isabel B. Wilson in memory of Alice Pratt Brown/The Bridgeman Art Library International/© 2010 Georgia O'Keeffe Museum/Artists Right Society (ARS), New York, 60; John & Lisa Merrill/Getty Images, 65; AP Images, 66, 89, 98 (bottom); Angela Arenal/iStockphoto, 71; John Loengard/Time Life Pictures/Getty Images, 73, 81, 92; Tony Vaccaro/Getty Images, 78; Eddy Risch/AP Images, 84